CATEGORIES OF REVOLUTIONARY MILITARY POLICY

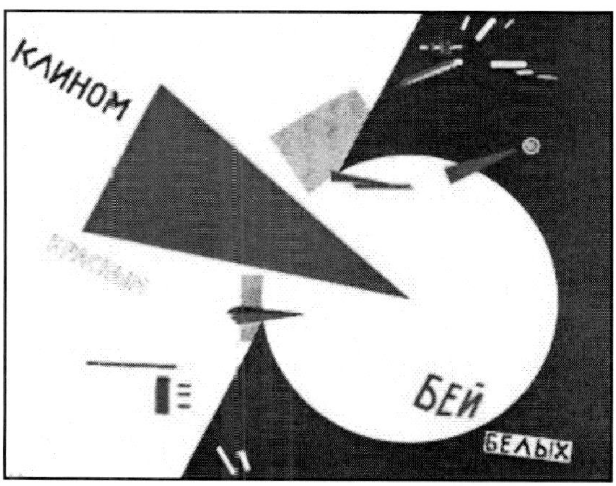

T. Derbent, April 2006

Categories of Revolutionary Military Policy
T. Derbent, April 2006
Translation by Kersplebedeb

ISBN 978-1-894946-43-8

First printing 2013
Printed in u.s.a.

This text is also available online at:
http://www.urbanguerilla.org/other/categories_derbent.php

Kersplebedeb can be contacted at:

Kersplebedeb
CP 63560
CCCP Van Horne
Montreal, Quebec
Canada
H3W 3H8

or email info@kersplebedeb.com
Visit the Kersplebedeb website at http://www.kersplebedeb.com

Guide to illustrations: page iv, *barricades in Prague, 1848;* page 7, *Naxalite guerilla, India;* page 15, *Nicaraguan revolution, 1979;* page 20, *Soviet partisans during Second World War;* page 23, *demonstration against police, Italy;* page 29, *peasant guerillas, China 1930s;* page 34, *member of Sendero Luminoso, Peru 2005;* page 36, *New People's Army, Mindanao;* page 38, *partisan during Second World War.*

Preface by Kersplebedeb

The following essay, by the Belgian revolutionary communist T. Derbent, is an unusual and valuable contribution to understanding, renewing, and rebuilding the revolutionary option.

The term "revolutionary" is used here to refer to something precise, namely action and reflection intended to bring about a revolution, a hegemonic change in the way society is organized, "bottom lining" the goals of liberation and building a new way of life for all.

Military policy is a prerequisite for revolutionaries—in the sense that, without it, there can be no successful revolution. Those who neglect it, who think away from it as we so often do, may have nice ideas, but they are neglecting a question that will be necessary to address if they are ever to put those nice ideas into practice in a durable manner. Indeed, would-be revolutionaries who have no military policy are not revolutionaries at all, but only more people with political opinions. While Derbent does not belabor this point, it underlies everything addressed here.

This essay is based on a talk given in Brussels at an event organized by the Bloc Marxiste-Léniniste in April 2006, and subsequently published in two parts in the Bloc ML's magazine *Clarté* (#5 May 2006 and #6 December 2006). It was subsequently translated into German, Greek, and Italian, being debated and discussed by comrades throughout Europe, mainly within the Marxist-Leninist tradition.

The present translation constitutes the first time this text is being made available to an English-reading audience—and specifically, to a North American one. The history of armed struggle in the united states and canada is necessarily different from that elsewhere; obviously, this is not Italy, or Algeria, or Nepal. The armed experience here has always been defined by the realities and contradictions of settler-colonialism, the tension between the ongoing anticolonial resistance and the fact that any movement here must find its way on terrain claimed by the colonizer's society.

Furthermore, as in any overview of such a dense area of knowledge and activity, this is not an exhaustive study. More to the point, it is a study with a specific goal: to introduce us to the concepts of military doctrine, and to explain how these have been used and misused by revolutionary forces. Although the author mentions objective factors, there is no discussion of historical materialism or broader historical patterns or dynamics; for example, the relationship between global changes in the means of production and distribution, and the inevitable calling up of completely new forms of struggle from military doctrine to individual tactics. Likewise, the author presupposes revolutionary organization, but doesn't have the space to go into what revolutionary class organization means in military practice (and vice-versa, dialectically).

Yet it would be a cop-out to hold this specificity against the text, or to dismiss Derbent's educational endeavor as a "European view" of little practical interest to those of us on Turtle Island. That is because this is not a "how-to-do-it," but rather a "how-to-study-it," paper. Surveying military experiences in various times and places—with particular attention paid to that period of the twentieth century marked by the presence of "real existing socialism" and ubiquitous anticolonial revolutions—in order to distill those elements, questions, and dilemmas that reoccur time and again; i.e., those that are universal. Laying out the background and consequences of already developed revolutionary policy considerations, in order to help us apply the lessons learned to our own context.

As such, this paper does not provide answers, it simply clarifies what some of the questions will be for those who choose to develop a revolutionary practice.

Derbent proceeds from the larger to the smaller, from the more general to the more specific. In this order, he defines and discusses revolutionary military policy (an overall military orientation & activity), military doctrine (a war plan), military development (organization of practical activity), the science of war (recognizing universal laws that always apply), the art of war (experience & mastery of the practice of warfare), strategy (a specific plan to achieve military goals in the existing overall situation), operational art (which connects strategy and tactics), and tactics (the means by which operations are carried out). The author examines how these different concepts are related to one another, how they have been articulated in different circumstances, and to what effect.

This is far from a rah-rah, inspirational pep talk relying on heroic examples of rebel armed struggle. Instead, it is of necessity fairly abstract and formal—otherwise it would be 440 instead of just 40 pages long. In particular, its terminology conforms to professional military usage. A graduate of the u.s. army's command & staff college at Fort Leavenworth would be at ease reading this paper, whose terminology and frame of mind would be familiar to them. While, on the other hand, a revolutionary who has never read Clausewitz along with Lenin and Mao's military writings ("Lessons of the 1905 Uprising," "Strategic Problems in the Anti-Japanese Guerrilla War," etc.) might find it difficult going.

All the more reason why it should be read, studied, discussed, and built upon by comrades here.

Categories of Revolutionary Military Policy
by T. Derbent

"It is true that at times the officers, exaggerating the relative impotence of intelligence, forget to use it." —Commander Charles de Gaulle, 1936

"Studying books is one way of learning; applying what we have learnt is another, even more important way... Our most important way is to learn to wage war by waging it..." —Mao Zedong, 1936

I. INTRODUCTION

Dear Comrades,

Louis XIV had the words *"ultima ratio regum"* engraved upon his cannons: *the final argument of kings.* Every social revolutionary project must think ahead to the question of armed confrontation with the forces of power and reaction. To put off making such a study because "the time is not right yet" for armed confrontation, amounts to making choices (political, strategic, organizational) which risk, at that point when "the time will be right" for armed confrontation, leaving the revolutionary forces powerless, vulnerable, with characteristics that will be totally inadequate. Choices which risk leaving them open to defeat.

Organizations that claim to be revolutionary but which refuse to develop a military policy *before the question of confrontation becomes a practical reality*, disqualify themselves as revolutionary forces. They are already acting as gravediggers of revolution, the quartermasters of stadiums and cemeteries.[1]

Therefore, the subject of this presentation is *revolutionary military policy*, which we can define as the analysis, the preparation, and the use of armed force in the service of the revolutionary objective.

The question of revolutionary military policy is being discussed once again. Whether it is a matter of studying the Protracted People's Wars led by Marxist-Leninist-Maoist type parties (in Peru, Nepal, India, or elsewhere), whether it is in re-examining the experiences of the urban guerilla in the imperialist metropoles over the past thirty years, or in other ways, debates about revolutionary military policy are experiencing a slight comeback. Even if the positions coming out of these debates remain very different (from the reaffirmation *sine variatur* of the insurrectionary principles of Lenin and the Comintern, to the crude appropriation of recent experiences in the dominated countries), this renewed interest in the question of revolutionary military policy is both good and necessary.

Yet revolutionary military thought remains anemic. Its propositions are the bastard progeny of historical methods (based on experience, which is based on historical antecedents with all the risks of dogmatism and conservatism that that implies) and philosophical methods (based on theory, which proceeds deductively with all the risks of subjectivism that that implies), methods that are used with no methodological or epistemological remove.

Witness the amorphous body of theory, with notions, for example, like "strategy," "military policy," "military theory," and "military

1 As well as the right-wing deviation that rejects thinking about strategy at this point in time, that reveals (and which ends up *bringing about*) the fact that revolutionary struggle has been reduced to the most trivial kind of protest, there is also a left-wing deviation that rejects the need to think about strategy beforehand. This deviation occurs amongst revolutionary forces which are anarchist, militarist, subjectivist, etc. and which claim that thinking about strategy "divides" revolutionaries who can only be united through action. In the heyday of focoism, some even claimed that thinking about strategy was a "bourgeois preoccupation."

doctrine" all employed as if they were interchangeable. The theoretical ambiguity is such that it permits, by means of an abuse of language, real political manipulations, as we saw when we analyzed the document from the (n)PCI *[the (New) Italian Communist Party—translator]* in our previous discussion.

This presentation is not about what today's revolutionary military policy *should* be. It is intended to be a tool to assist in a rigorous, methodical, and scientific evaluation of revolutionary military policy.

The limits of this presentation are plain to see. In and of itself, it is not tied to any particular line, but it is dealing with a field where categories are based on analyses and political-theoretical choices. The old debate about whether or not such a thing as proletarian military science exists is an example of this problem.[2] Between the left-wing deviation, which denies that there is anything valid in the body of military science elaborated under the bourgeois regime, and the right-wing deviation which prostates itself before bourgeois military thought, there is a narrow path which has yet to be made clear.

What's more, as soon as it abandons its basis in precise strategic thought—meaning its basis in a concrete analysis of a concrete situation, which means connected to political practice—then the author's efforts will amount to nothing but abstract theory. But to the degree that this presentation is a tool, it will be how it is used, that is to say its application in concrete situations, that will allow us to identify and get rid of those categories that are of only academic interest. As Maurice Biraud said, in the film *Un taxi pour Tobrouk*, *"an uneducated person who walks will go farther than two intellectuals who remain seated."*

Right?

We're off...

2 This was a debate that initially involved Trotsky opposing Stalin and Vorochilov in 1918, and then Frounzé in 1921.

II. OBJECTIVE FACTORS, SUBJECTIVE FACTORS

The first thing to note regarding revolutionary military policy is its inherent limits. We know that the counter-insurgency command is happy to draw upon the ideas of Colonel Trinquier. But these ideas are crudely antidialectical, and conceive of revolution as the result of a conspiracy consisting of two types of person: the "agents" of subversion and the "masses" who they manipulate. According to Trinquier, revolutionary crises break out at the point that the underground command decides: that's when it plays its hand.

In fact, revolutionary crises break out due to a combination of objective and subjective factors. More often than not, the revolutionary forces are surprised by the rush of events. Such was the case in the crisis of 1905, which caught the Bolshevik party by surprise and without any military structure; it was the case in 1917 (we know how hard Lenin had to fight within the party—especially against Zinoviev and Kamenev—to move towards insurrection); the magnitude of success at Santa Clara (September-December 1959) came as a great surprise to the Castroist guerillas; the same with the general insurrection in Managua in 1979. Preparations and actions by the party are indispensable for a revolutionary victory, but they are never enough to explain the revolutionary phenomenon. A revolution is first and foremost the expression of a society's internal contradictions. This is why Lenin held the position that no insurrection was possible if the ruling classes were not already in a severe political crisis, unable to govern as before, and if the oppressed classes were not pushed to revolt by a decline in their living conditions. The failure of counter-revolutionary subversive wars shows how important these socio-historical conditions are (failure in that they have never brought a counter-revolution to power by means of "people's" war, though they may have contributed to the process by destroying the economy in Nicaragua and Mozambique).

III. MILITARY DOCTINE

The first thing the Party[3] must decide upon is its *military doctrine*. The military doctrine is the articulation of opinions held by the Party as to its political evaluation of the problems related to the war in question, the Party's attitude towards this war, its definition, the organization and preparation of the Party's forces, the choice of its strategy and methods. It is, to use the Clausewitzian term, its war plan.

It follows that what military doctrine is chosen will depend on the socio-historical situation. At the time of the Nazi invasion, the European Communist Parties (CPs) were "configured" for a doctrine of "internal" (national) class struggle and so they had decided upon a proletarian-insurrectionary strategy, i.e. primarily legal parties supplemented by clandestine military structures. This setup was not suited to the new conditions and led to heavy initial losses (the Belgian Communist Party was decapitated by Operation "Sonnenwende"), and the CPs were then forced to improvise a practice of protracted people's war.[4]

The Party's military doctrine can be defined as the answer to the following questions:

1. Who is (and who will be) the enemy?

This is based not only on an analysis of the State and its forces, but also on a class analysis of society (to define the possible attitudes of the intermediate classes), an analysis of the international situation (to determine

3 Whether or not a class Party is necessary for the social revolution is a critically important question, but one that is beyond the scope of this presentation. As is the equally important question of whether (if we deem the Party to be necessary) establishing such a Party is a necessary precondition for commencing the armed confrontation. For the sake of convenience I am using the term "Party" here, but if one prefers one could understand this as meaning "force," "organization," "movement," etc.

4 The achievements of the CPs once they embarked upon this new path were remarkable: they were able to militarily organize large masses of people despite fierce repression. What limits the use of these examples for the future is the fact that the CPs were emphasizing National Liberation rather than Socialist Revolution: this won them support from large layers of the petit bourgeoisie and the peasantry that would have been hostile to the dictatorship of the proletariat.

how much support the State can expect from the imperialist bourgeoisie as well as what forces might intervene to assist the revolutionary camp), etc.

2. What is (and will be) the nature of the war to come?
Will it be a "pure" class struggle right from the very get-go, with the proletariat facing the bourgeoisie in a struggle to the death? Will it be a struggle in which the class dimension is associated with a national dimension? And if so, then will some process unite these two dimensions or will they occur in two different stages (a national liberation stage where it is "only" a matter of getting the occupation forces to leave and a social stage where it is a matter of destroying the reactionary forces)? Will it be a struggle with both a democratic revolution stage and a proletarian revolution stage? And if so, then will these be two separate things or will there be two distinct stages (a stage where the proletarian forces can count on large sections of the middle classes joining the revolutionary camp, and a stage where the proletariat will have to fight on its own to establish its dictatorship)?

3. What are the objectives and the missions that the armed forces will undertake as a result?
Destroy the enemy's armed forces? Make the human and/or material cost of the war too high for the enemy? A combination of the above (for example: destroy the domestic bourgeoisie's armed forces and discourage possible foreign intervention by acquiring the means necessary to make the war too costly for them)? Limit armed activity within the nation's borders or integrate it within a regional strategy? Etc.

4. What are (and will be) the armed forces necessary at first, and what kind of organizational and technical developments will be required to reach this stage? What will be the armed forces necessary in the later stages of the war, and what military, organizational and technical developments and what kind of internal process will this require?

It is not just a matter of numbers, but also of what kind of forces these will be—militias (of workers and/or peasants) and/or regular units—and of their relationship to the Party—organic unity between the political and the military or the (relative) separation of the armed wing, for instance in the form of a Red Army.

5. How should the Party prepare?
Not only in terms of its internal organization (clandestinity, choices about internal process in terms of Party democracy and discipline, militarization of some of its cadres and militants, separation into cells, creation of an ad hoc security and intelligence apparatus, etc.), but also in terms of bringing together different resources, etc.

6. What will be the strategy and the methods used to wage and win this war?
Guerilla warfare? Insurrection? A coup? etc. This must be based upon an analysis of the politico-military balance of power (objective and subjective factors, such as the will to fight). It must also be based upon an analysis of the impact of geographic, economic, social and other factors on the ability of the forces in question to move, to strike, to gather information, to hide, to concentrate their forces, to disperse, to fall back, to communicate, etc.

IV. MILITARY DEVELOPMENT

The Party's military doctrine effects its *military development*, which includes all aspects relating to its military force:

1. Organizational Aspects

In the case of a strategic decision in favor of a "Fighting Party," a "Politico-Military Party,"[5] or a "Militarized Party"[6]: thought must be given to how the Party's structures are set up in order to tailor them to both political and military work.

- In the case of a strategic decision in favor of a Party controlling a distinct military force[7] (an embryonic Red Army), this distinct structure needs to be created, or, at the very least, thought must be given as to how to prepare for its creation (selection of cadres, etc.).
- In all cases: either bringing the Party underground or preparing to bring it underground; training cadres for underground work; establishing a clandestine structure (safehouses, documents, communication); adopting security measures (separation into cells, etc.).

2. Military Aspects

Acquiring the military resources (weapons, equipment) required or beneficial for the military doctrine, and/or making plans and preparing methods and connections to make these resources available at the appropriate time[8] (for example: plans to attack a barracks); providing all cadres with an introduction to military questions and providing military training to specific cadres.

---

5 The theory held by the European fighting communist school of thought.

6 The theory held by one section of the Marxist-Leninist-Maoist school of thought.

7 The theory held by the other communist schools of thought.

8 The *appropriate* time is not necessarily the *chosen* time: it can be imposed by the enemy's initiative, such as the Nazi coup in 1933 which pre-empted the insurrection the KPD had been preparing.

3. Economic and Logistical Aspects
Acquiring the economic and logistical resources (money, housing, vehicles, means of communication, of making false papers, etc.) required or beneficial for the military doctrine, and/or making plans and preparing methods and connections to make these resources available at the appropriate time.

4. Political Aspects
Implementing a program of politically preparing the Party's militants and cadres for the war defined as necessary or desirable by the military doctrine.

5. Scientific and Technical Aspects
Acquiring the scientific and technical resources required and/or available (to produce weapons and equipment required by combat and clandestinity, to intercept enemy communications and to protect one's own communications, etc.) defined as necessary or desirable by the military doctrine, or updating plans and methods in order to ensure that these resources will be available at the appropriate time; training cadres.

6. Ideological and Moral Aspects
The ideological and moral preparation of militants, of the sympathetic masses and of the masses in general, for the war considered necessary or desirable by the military doctrine. An example of this would be the way in which solidarity work with revolutionary prisoners can contribute to the ideological struggle in favor of armed conflict.

7. Internal Process: Discipline and Democracy
Adopting an internal process with forms of discipline and democracy defined as necessary or desirable by the military doctrine. An example of this would be the choice made by the Vietnamese communists in the time of the Resistance to adopt the system known as the "three great democracies." This allowed them to develop the initiative, the dynamism, and the

creative faculties of cadres and combatants, to reinforce the cohesion and the solidarity of the armed forces and to increase their combat strength:

- Political Democracy: in base units, to regularly hold democratic meetings, military assemblies where combatants as well as cadres can voice their opinions about everything relating to combat, work as well as training, education, and life in the unit; the cadres have the right to criticize the combatants, but the combatants also have the right to criticize the cadres.
- Military Democracy: in the field and training alike (conditions permitting), to hold democratic meetings in order to communicate the operational plan to everyone, to allow people to use their initiative, and to work together to find the means to overcome difficulties in order to accomplish the task at hand.[9]
- Economic Democracy: combatants and cadres alike have the right to participate in the administration and improvement of material conditions in an "open book" system.

Revolutionary armed forces normally adopt a system of *strict discipline, freely consented to*. Discipline that is freely consented to, because it builds upon the political consciousness of the cadres and the combatants and is largely maintained through a process of ongoing education and persuasion. This system is such that everyone is motivated to respect it and to help each other to observe it. Strict discipline means that all members of the army, without exception, cadres as well as combatants, superiors as well as subordinates, must respect it to the letter and nobody is exempt.

Democracy and discipline should serve to reinforce the military power of the revolutionary forces. From this perspective, the difference

9 In bourgeois armies, soldiers only has the right to know what is strictly necessary in order to accomplish their mission. They obey orders because they were trained to do so. Murat didn't bother to explain anything to his guards, he simply shouted "The direction: my asshole!" and shoved their head into their objective.

between democracy and "democratism" is essential; the former reinforces military power, the latter weakens it.[10]

V. THE SCIENCE OF WAR

The *science of war* aids the Party in elaborating its military doctrine. This is the unified body of knowledge dealing with the psychological and physical aspects of combat. Its contents are organized around two basic laws:

1. War is subordinate to political objectives;
2. The result of a conflict depends on the relationship of military power (numbers and quality—courage, discipline and self-discipline, motivation, training—of combatants, quality and quantity of war matériel, capacity and character of the leadership, etc.), as well as political, moral, technical, social, and economic forces.

The science of war can be divided into four categories:

1. The study of war, including the history *of wars* (or more precisely, so far as we are concerned, the history of civil and revolutionary wars).
2. The *laws of war*, meaning those *principles* which it is imperative to apply on all levels (strategic, tactical, etc.), and those *rules* whose application, while desirable, is not always possible in conditions that make them worthwhile.[11] Meaning:

---

10 The Spanish Civil War provides numerous examples of the disastrous effects of "democratism." For instance, at the battles of Alto de Leon and Somosierre in July-August 1935 where the militias refused to attack without first holding a vote... The militias enjoyed superiority in numbers, motivation, equipment and position, but despite all this they were badly beaten by the regular units led by fascist officers. The question of "democratism" was at the center of Lin Piao's attack against General Ho Long during the Cultural Revolution.

11 For example, *initiative* is only worth having if one is able to keep it: the Paris Commune took the initiative against Versailles, but at the first setback it became clear that it did not have the means to keep it. By the same token, *surprise* is only useful if one is able to exploit it, etc.

⇒The principle that *the means should be proportional to the goal.*

⇒The principle of *freedom of action*, which requires that forces be deployed so as to be able to pursue their goal without offering a hold for enemy forces, and which contains certain rules such as bringing forces together (enabling them to engage in combat as needed); security (constantly seeking intelligence on the enemy, active and passive security measures, etc.); initiative; mobility; hiding one's intentions from the enemy; preventing the enemy from reacting; establishing reserves; etc.

⇒The principle of an *economy of force* (in other words: getting the most out of one's resources by the active and intelligent use of all forces), which also contains certain rules: bringing together the greatest possible resources at the point where the stakes are highest, by cutting back on secondary fronts;[12] concentrating the use of forces as much as possible; coordinating all resources in order to multiply their respective effectiveness; choosing the right moment; choosing the right place; surprise (strategic, tactical,

12 The universality of the principle of *economy of force* is what gives the guerilla its strategic value. The guerilla (and the urban guerilla even more than the rural guerilla) allows for an optimal use of weak forces, and obliges the enemy to deploy countless forces in order to guard potential targets—and in this way, obliges it to abandon this principle. But if by definition the guerilla benefits from the advantage provided by the *economy of force*, the principle can and must be applied with care by the guerilla, in the positioning and use of their own forces. When an insurrection (or a coup) enjoys the necessary conditions of surprise, it too benefits from this principle, which explains how weak forces, if used intelligently, can take apart a numerically superior enemy: insurrectionary forces seize certain areas but temporarily leave others in the hands of enemy units, they concentrate their forces at decisive points and battles while the enemy, taken by surprise, has some of its troops at rest, etc. All the same, the principle of *economy of force* has its limits, and there are discrepancies in the relationship of forces that it cannot overcome.

technical through the use of new methods or by an original or unexpected use of old methods); speed (which extends the effect of surprise and guarantees freedom of action); continuity of efforts; exploiting the enemy's lack of preparedness; etc.

3. The theoretical basis of the Party's preparation for war.
4. The art of war.

VI. THE ART OF WAR

Unlike the science of war to which it belongs, the *art of war* is not a rigorous body of knowledge about phenomena and their laws. As a concrete activity (not a speculative one), the art of war never encounters two identical situations: neither the means nor the enemy nor the terrain nor the socio-economic conditions are ever the same. What's more, war is not just a confrontation between material forces, it is also a confrontation between wills, between moral forces that often radically modify the value of the material forces.

The principal aspects of the art of war are:

1. Strategy
2. The art of operations (or *operational art*)
3. Tactics
4. Logistics (relative to movement, positioning, and supplying the armed forces)
5. Organization (relating to the organization and preparation of matériel and people)

The art of war resides in mastering and articulating these different aspects and their specific characteristics. (For instance, being aware of the tactical importance of establishing reserves given that combat often proceeds as a series of engagements, even though strategy demands strict respect for the economy of forces, meaning their full use where they might make a critical difference.)

VII. STRATEGY

Strategy consists of implementing the concepts and recommendations that emerge from the military doctrine. To do this, it addresses both military and non-military problems, it transforms the Party's *military strength* (a quantitative concept) into *military power* (a dynamic, non-quantifiable concept), and it takes the place of military doctrine as soon as combat begins.

Therefore, strategy has:

1. This definition: the proper use of combat in pursuit of the aims of the war.
2. This starting point: the will to obtain the greatest result, as quickly as possible and with the least cost, by efficient use of force—strategy therefore obeys the law of economy of force.
3. These means: Successful operations (made possible by the correctness of the strategic analysis and obtained by revolutionary forces mastering operational art and tactics) which are then exploited militarily, politically (propaganda, etc.), and organizationally (integration of new combatants, etc.).
4. These principles: the (absolute) importance of superiority at key points (one cannot "attack everything" or "defend everything"); the (relative) importance of surprise and subterfuge; keeping the goal in proportion to the forces and obstacles.
5. This goal: objectives that should lead to peace, which in the case of revolutionary war means destroying the enemy forces and breaking the enemy's will to fight.

Nothing guarantees that the means will advance towards the goal; not every successful operation is necessarily a good thing on the strategic level (for instance, one that leads to an escalation that the revolutionary camp is not prepared to handle—foreign intervention for example). Strategic analysis determines what operations should be carried out, and in what framework.

Other than the principles and rules of the art of war, of which strategy is a key part, strategic analysis is based on its own criteria. These include:

1. The laws that govern warfare. Listed above, they are objective and apply equally to both sides.
2. The nature and characteristics of the war to be waged; the distribution of forces (social, military, political, etc., actual as well as potential, in both qualitative and quantitative terms); its prospective duration, intensity, and scope; the possibilities of foreign intervention (friendly or hostile); geographic and social conditions, etc.
3. The Party's preparedness for war.
4. Material and technical assets (military resources, techniques, information, cadres, combatants, scientists).
5. Leadership of the forces.
6. The choices the enemy is likely to make, for the strategic domain consists of the belligerents' actions and reactions.

On this basis, strategic analysis means:

1. A meticulous calculation of the risks involved; specifically, this means anticipating how as the revolution progresses there will be a qualitative escalation on the part of the counter-revolution (torture, extrajudicial executions, etc.);
2. Always keeping operations perfectly in line with the political-military goal (i.e., not reacting on the basis of prestige);
3. Preparing a fallback position;
4. Resolution once the action is initiated;
5. Being flexible about what methods/resources to use when faced with unforeseen developments.

VIII. THE GENERAL PRINCIPLES OF REVOLUTIONARY STRATEGY

What are the *general principles of revolutionary strategy*? We can list five:

1. It is based on the primacy of the political over the military (and this goes beyond the general principle of subordinating military options to political objectives: it is a matter of politics being primary across the board; as such, the political education of revolutionaries is more important than their military education; the political-ideological impact of an operation can be more important than its material effect, military operations can be suspended but political work must never stop, etc.);
2. It is based on the primacy of people over things;[13]
3. It is based on the primacy of the interior (what is happening within the country, what is happening within the class) over the exterior;
4. It is always concerned with its connection to the popular masses;
5. Regardless of the main form of struggle adopted (insurrection, guerilla, etc.), no form of struggle is neglected: mass struggle (strikes, demonstrations), guerilla warfare, traditional warfare, sabotage, legal struggles, psychological warfare, covert warfare, terrorism, and insurrectionary movements.
6. Its goal is the total destruction of the enemy's armed forces. Unlike other forms of war, the revolutionary war is a war of annihilation which cannot be ended by making a deal or holding peace talks with the enemy.

13 In China's People's Liberation Army, these theses were spelled out in the system known as "the four primacies": primacy of people over things, of political work over other activities, of ideological work over other forms of political work, and of living ideas over booklearning within ideological work.

IX. THE PRINCIPAL REVOLUTIONARY STRATEGIES

To speak a bit more concretely, we will quickly go over the principal revolutionary strategies that have been theorized since the proletariat's entrance on the historical scene. I have counted eleven, though this is somewhat arbitrary as certain categories could be subdivided to make new ones.

1. The Blanquist Insurrectionary Strategy.

The most advanced example of this strategy is the Blanquist strategy, theorized in the *Manual for Armed Insurrection*.[14] A small group of armed conspirators (between 500 and 800 in the May 12 uprising in 1839) strikes when it thinks the people are subjectively ready for insurrection, acting in the place of the unorganized proletariat. They take control of the armories and distribute weapons, striking at the head of the political power structure and its agents of repression (attack on the police headquarters), systematically erecting barricades and organizing the masses who rally to the insurrection. On a tactical level, Blanqui relied heavily on barricades—a decision which was correctly criticized by Engels. The passive tactic of barricades was pursued by the revolutionary proletariat up until 1848; the only way it could have succeeded would have been if large numbers of soldiers from the bourgeois army had decided to desert and cross over to the insurrectionary camp.

2. The Strategy of the Insurrectionary General Strike.

Bakunin's legacy (whether acknowledged or not), which aimed to bring about the abolition of the State through a single collective action, preferably a general strike. Such an insurrection would be set off as a result of the spontaneity of the masses. According to this strategy, the insurrectionary

14 The way in which Lenin denied accusations that he was a "Blanquist" should not lead us to overlook the fact that the Blanquist *taking up of arms* is the intermediate step between the Babouvian conspiracy and the Leninist insurrection. The "Blanquist" epithet that Plekhanov and Martov threw at Lenin had very little to do with true Blanquism. What it meant, in the political vocabulary of the day, was that one was in favor of conspiratorial rather than mass action.

general strike will occur when the masses are subjectively ready, and this subjective disposition will allow all the objective questions (military, organizational) to be easily resolved thanks to the masses' revolutionary creativity. This strategy also relies on a large-scale breakdown of bourgeois power, this too being due to the subjective disposition of the masses (mass desertions from the army, etc.). This strategy was proposed anew in the interwar period by the Revolutionary Syndicalists, and has also reappeared at times amongst the "mao-spontex" and within the Bordiguist ultraleft.

3. The Strategy of Exemplary Terrorism.
Practiced by a tendency within the anarchist movement and by the Russian populists. It is based on either the actions of individuals or of a secret organization—and is always lacking any organic connection to the masses. Their only way of connecting to the masses is through the example their actions provide, or the attitude of their militants when faced with repression, and, eventually, some declarations. The terrorist strategy was able to hit reaction at its highest points, provoking terror amongst the enemy and winning the admiration of the masses, but it has never been able to translate these factors into forces able to overthrow a government. Historically, this strategy has only ever produced failures: one does not "wake up" the revolutionary layers of the masses without organizing them.

4. The Leninist-Comintern Insurrectionary Strategy.
First implemented in October 1917 and meticulously theorized thereafter (notably in the collective work *Armed Insurrection* signed "Neuberg"), this was the strategy adopted by the Communist parties in the 1920s and '30s. It integrates and systematizes the analyses of Marx and Engels (and the lessons of experiences like 1905) by bestowing a central role on the vanguard Party which will work to bring together the elements necessary for a successful revolution (raising the revolutionary consciousness of the masses, political and military organization of the masses notably by creating a Red Guard, training and equipping shock troops and using

these instead of barricades, setting up an insurrectionary headquarters, drafting battle plans, determining the right time to strike, etc.). This strategy met with major failures in Germany (1923), China (1927), Asturia (1934), Brazil (1935), and elsewhere.

5. The Strategy of Protracted People's War

It has three stages: a guerilla stage, strategically defensive (though tactically very active, consisting of non-stop initiatives); a stage of strategic equilibrium; a strategically offensive stage during which the revolutionary forces are able to wage a war of movement and a (supplementary) war of position. The specific principles of Protracted People's War were outlined as follows by Mao Zedong:

- First attack dispersed and isolated enemy forces, then attack the more important forces.
- First establish liberated zones in the countryside, encircle the cities by the countryside, first take the small cities, then take the large ones.
- Make sure to greatly outnumber the enemy in combat (the strategy is about how to fight one against ten, the tactic is to fight ten against one).[15]
- Ensure combatants have a high level of political consciousness, so that they will be superior in endurance, courage, and sense of self-sacrifice.
- Make sure to have the support of the people, take care to respect their interests.
- Make sure that captured enemies pass over to the revolutionary camp.

15 This principle was theorized by Mao Zedong in *On Protracted War* and by Zhu De in *On the Anti-Japanese War*. But Giap and the rest of the Viet Minh leadership did not agree, and in any case considered it ill-suited to the Vietnamese situation. The small numbers of Viet Minh forces often led them to engage with equal numbers of combatants on the tactical level; surprise, better knowledge of the terrain, and the operational quality of their troops (the degree of combat preparedness and revolutionary heroism) being enough to make the difference.

- Use the time between battles to improve, train, and educate yourselves.

Victorious in Yugoslavia, Albania, China, and Indochina, this strategy has met with major failures, notably in Greece (1945-49) and Malaysia (1948-60).

6. The Strategy of the Coup

Relies on the relationship of forces being extremely favorable to the revolutionary party. For instance, in Prague 1948, we can note the presence of the Soviet Army, the strength and prestige of the Communist Party, the existence of popular militias (15,000-18,000 armed workers), the near total infiltration of the National Security Corps and of several army units, etc. This strategy has the advantage of being infinitely more economical than those which necessitate armed conflict. It can even maintain the semblance of legality, which enables the political neutralization of certain intermediate social strata. The coup generally results from an opportunity provided by extraordinary historic circumstances rather than a revolutionary strategy theorized as such or elaborated as a model. Nonetheless, in the Third World in the 1960s and '70s it was systematically applied by young progressive officers connected in various ways to the Soviet Union.

7. The Strategy of Armed Electoralism

Based on the theory that a partial seizure of power is possible by legal means (the condition being that a large mass struggle exists to guarantee democratic rights) and that this partial seizure of power will provide the revolutionary movement with the tools that, in conjunction with the resources of the revolutionary forces themselves, will be enough to ensure the advance of the revolutionary process and to hold in check the reactionary counter-offensive (military coup or foreign intervention). Organizations that adopt this strategy outfit themselves with a military potential to ensure a seizure of power which is actually based on legal methods. General Pinochet did a lot to discredit this strategic hypothesis, which had already experienced a bloody failure with the decimation of the Austrian *Schutzbund* in 1934.

8. The Focoist Strategy

A theory based on systematizing the specific experiences[16] of guerillas active in the late 1950s and early 1960s in Latin America (including Cuba). It makes establishing and developing a mobile rural base of guerilla operations into the central aspect of the revolutionary process. Focoism is not intended to be universally applicable, and was largely based on ideas about the duality of Latin American society (the capitalist city and the feudal countryside), of the impossibility of establishing liberated zones as was done in Indochina, etc. The guerilla's mobile bases are supposed to develop into a people's army, to encircle the cities until the regime is finished off by an insurrectionary general strike in the urban centers. Prior to this coup de grace, the proletariat's role is limited to supporting the rural guerilla.

---

16 This basing a theory on the systematization of specific experiences (often the result of empirical experience, and the product or expression of the weaknesses of the Latin American revolutionary movement) has been the source of a lot of confusion. It allowed the most important theoretician of focoism, Regis Debray, to reject Leninist-Maoist ideas (such as the role of the class Party) despite these having been insisted upon by the person who, according to Debray, embodied the focoist "revolution in the revolution": Che Guevara.

9. The Neo-Insurrectionary Strategy

Emerged following the success of the Sandinista revolution in Nicaragua. In the wake of this victory many revolutionary forces either wholly or partially abandoned the Protracted People's War strategy—a strategy that in some cases they had been pursuing for decades—in order to try to bring things to a head by calling for urban uprisings. This was the case with the New People's Army, led by the Communist Party of the Philippines,[17] until its 1992 rectification campaign brought it back to the concept of Protracted People's War.

10. The P.A.S.S. Strategy (Politico-Military Fighting Strategy) of Combined Revolutionary Warfare (CRW)

Defined and implemented by Mahir Çayan and the founders of the People's Liberation Party/Front of Turkey, and adopted by several organizations in the 1970s and '80s (Dev Yol, Dev Sol, MLSPB, THKP-People's Revolutionary Vanguards, etc.). According to this strategy, the guerilla remains primary up until the stage of traditional warfare, and other forms of struggle (political, economic, democratic, and ideological) are subordinate to it. The PASS strategy is divided into three stages:

- The creation of the urban guerilla (it is easier to build up a fighting force in a city, armed actions there will resonate more, the social terrain is better disposed to accept and understand high-level actions).
- The guerilla spreads throughout the entire country, and alongside the urban guerilla a rural guerilla is established. (This will play a more important role because a rural unit can

17 It was primarily in Mindanao in the early 1980s that the NPA rejected the strategy of Protracted People's War and in a subjectivist manner forced a transition from the "defensive" phase to the phase of the "strategic counter-offensive." Small mobile NPA units that were firmly anchored amongst the people were prematurely combined into battalions within which PCP cadres were supposed to take on military responsibilities for which they were insufficiently prepared. The Party's clandestine structures came out of this severely weakened, and the major NPA battalions, which were easy to identify, suffered heavy losses from an enemy that was far from being on the verge of defeat.

withdraw and develop by progressively integrating peasants on an ongoing basis, while the urban guerilla, which must scatter to clandestine bases following each action, cannot hope to establish an ongoing relationship with the masses or develop into a people's army.)

- The transformation of the guerilla forces into a regular army.

11. The Strategy of Protracted Revolutionary Warfare

Defined and implemented by fighting communist organizations in Europe. Based on the principles of Maoist Protracted People's War but with the major difference of giving up on any form of rural guerilla (and with it the idea of the countryside encircling the cities), by replacing liberated zones with clandestine networks in mass organizations (trade unions, etc.), by the greater importance given to acts of armed propaganda, and by adopting new organizational relationships between Party- and military-oriented work (to the point, in some cases, of rejecting the traditional separation between Communist Party and Red Army and developing the idea of the Fighting Party, justified by the new political quality of armed struggle), etc.

This highly schematic list is not meant as a "catalog" from which one has to choose some ready-made formula. Every particular situation calls for a particular response. Each concrete case will contain elements from different strategies, either due to inertia (the survival of old methods), or alternately because the struggle causes new methods to crop up, methods that will only be theorized and systematized after the fact. The most we can hope for is that this list serve as a guide.

It will be noted that these strategies can be divided into two broad categories: those that seek to bring things to a head in one battle (insurrectionary strategies) and those that seek to settle matters through a series of battles and campaigns (guerilla strategies).[18] Each of these broad categories comes with its own deviation: a right-wing deviation in the case of insurrectionary strategies, which are sometimes adopted by forces affected by opportunism as a way of postponing the confrontation with those in power; a left-wing deviation in the case of guerilla strategies, which are sometimes adopted by forces affected by subjectivism in order to avoid doing the work required to root themselves in the class.

X. REVOLUTIONARY STRATEGY AND DOGMA

In and of themselves, neither the insurrectionary nor the guerilla school of strategy is necessarily dogmatic, nor is either one necessarily undogmatic.

Each school has "its own" dogmatic adherents, and what stands

18 In the debate we had previously (about the document from the (n)PCI), we had to consider the idea that the Bolshevik Party had been pursuing a people's war strategy "without knowing it"—the 1917 insurrection corresponding to the third phase (the generalized offensive) of this strategy. This is a very interesting idea, but we have not been able to pursue the kind of historical investigation that would be required to evaluate it. Amongst the questions that would have to be answered for us: Between 1905 and 1917, did any aspect of the Bolshevik Party's line parallel that of protracted war? If so, did that aspect significantly contribute to the Party's development? The Bolshevik Party did engage in armed struggle (sheltering militants, liquidating informants, fundraising operations), but what was the objective and subjective reality (the importance that this had in the eyes of cadres, of militants, of the masses)? Did any armed activities persist between 1908 and 1917?

out in each case is that dogmatic interpretations of the strategic option are the product of forces which are developing an opportunist practice behind their warlike rhetoric.

1. Regarding Insurrection

Amongst true-believers in "insurrection theology," the latter is somewhat like the horizon: the more they move towards it, the further it moves away. By separating the medium-term objectives from the (supposed) long-term objective—armed insurrection—they are developing a line that might strengthen the Party and its influence in the medium term as regards Party-oriented work, the organization of advanced workers, tactics in mass struggles, etc.—but which objectively hinders the emergence of those objective and subjective conditions necessary for the revolutionary crisis that will set off the insurrection.

2. Regarding Protracted War

Some "Maoists" propose aping Mao's Protracted People's War in conditions (politico-historical, socio-economic, geographic, etc.) that are far removed from those in the dominated countries, and then they constantly put off initiating the armed struggle with the pretext that the supposedly necessary "preconditions" are lacking. At times certain substitutes for armed struggle will appear, for example borrowing spectacular forms of propaganda (a hammer and sickle in flames on a mountainside overlooking a city) used by forces (in the case of this example, the PCP) that actually do wage armed struggle. That is when we see this real abuse of language occur, whereby declarations are made that a group is waging a "people's war" even though it is not carrying out any armed actions.[19]

19 This is not only a problem amongst dogmatists. We experienced the same thing in our previous debate: the (n)PCI claims to be in the "first phase" of people's war, and yet not only does it not carry out any armed actions, but what's more it distances itself from those forces that are doing so (i.e. the Red Brigades). Depending on how much faith one has in the honesty of the (n)PCI, this is either an abuse of language (for as Clausewitz has shown, war is defined by the used of armed force), or it is a political scam.

XI. UNIVERSAL AND SPECIFIC CHARACTERISTICS

Turning away from dogmatism means:

1. Establishing military policy (and in doing so, making strategic choices) based on a rigorous analysis of history and of the current objective and subjective conditions. This analysis can lead either to the position that one strategic option is universally applicable (in other words, that either insurrection or protracted warfare should always and everywhere be adopted as the sole revolutionary strategy applicable),[20] or to the position that the choice between insurrection and protracted warfare should be based on objective circumstances. To hold that a strategic option is universally applicable is not inherently dogmatic. It can be, but it can also be the product of exhaustive, rigorous, and honest investigation, an attempt to identify the laws of history in order to act upon it. This is a method in line with the principles of historical materialism. So long as the only revolutionary victories had been the Paris Commune and the October Revolution, historical analysis naturally tended to view armed insurrection as the only way possible. The revolutionary victories in China and Indochina shook up this supposed historical proof. Distinguishing the exception from the rule[21] is an absolutely necessary exercise, but one that is beyond the scope of this presentation.
2. Once the strategy has been decided upon, turning away from dogmatism means facing the question of the universal and specific aspects of the strategic option chosen.

---

20 This does not mean that one should not take advantage of exceptional historical circumstances, such as occurred in Czechoslovakia in 1948.

21 Was the October 1917 insurrection the historical exception that only managed to succeed due to the extreme weakness of the regime? Or were the protracted wars in China and Indochina the exceptions that only succeeded due to the critically important anti-feudal and national liberation dimensions to their struggles?

1. For Insurrection

The Neuberg Comintern manual provides an excellent example: armed insurrection is presented as a "necessity" and a "destiny" of the class struggle. At no point does Neuberg's work question the insurrectionary strategy; all of the criticisms it makes (which are both numerous and interesting) concern errors implementing it (bad timing, insufficient or badly deployed forces, lack of coordination, etc.). It is assumed that the insurrectionary option has been "proven," and on this basis each concrete experience (Hamburg in 1923, Canton in 1927, Reval in 1934, etc.) is studied in order to aid revolutionaries in adapting the strategy to their own socio-historical circumstances: over here it will be necessary to precede the insurrection with a general strike, over there it will be necessary to initiate it by surprise, etc.

2. For Protracted War

The question of the universal and specific characteristics of protracted war has been most thoroughly examined by President Gonzalo. In his view, when Mao Zedong established the principles of people's war he provided the proletariat with its military line, its theory, and its military practice, *"universally, meaning applicable everywhere based on concrete conditions."* Regarding the criticism that this recognition of the universal applicability of revolutionary warfare is a sign of dogmatism, President Gonzalo's answer is that concrete circumstances give rise to different kinds of tactics, struggle, and organization. He listed three such specificities in Peru: *first,* the importance of the struggle in the cities alongside the struggle in the countryside (reflecting the importance of cities in Latin America); *second,* the fact of having been able and obliged to establish forms of popular power in the liberated zones prior to the defeat of the armed forces (because of their late entry on the scene in 1982, long after the police forces had been routed); *third,* the militarization of the Party.[22]

22 "Prachanda Path" is the Nepali equivalent of "Gonzalo Thought." (Translator's note: recall that this text was written in 2006.)

XII. BASES OF SUPPORT, GUERILLA ZONES, AND LIBERATED TERRITORIES

Unlike the question of universal and specific characteristics, the question of "bases of support" only applies to guerilla strategies. We will begin by examining the different categories.

1. The Guerilla Zone

This is a geographic category: the area in which the guerilla is active, where it moves and is active.

2. The Base of Support

This category is both geographic and politico-social. It is a zone where the enemy is present (or which it can penetrate with ease) but where revolutionary counter-power also exists. The revolutionary party is firmly anchored amongst the masses and the guerilla enjoys support (recruits, supplies, shelter, information, etc.). The social relationships are still those of the old society, but the balance of power between classes has changed: the people's demands are reinforced by support from the revolutionary armed forces.[23]

3. The Stationary or Stable Base of Support

A given area in which political-military control exists, where the regime's institutions have been driven out, and which will be defended against enemy armed forces. It is the intermediate level between a base of support and a liberated zone.

---

23 So it was in China and Indochina, where the Communist Party put limits on sharecropping, usury, etc. in order to defend the interests of impoverished peasants. So also, today in Colombia, where narcotraffickers operating in the FARC's bases of support are obliged to pay peasants a guaranteed price for coca (as well as a tax to the FARC), while in areas controlled by the paramilitaries the narcotraffickers use white terror (starting with the systematic elimination of peasant trade unionists) in order to impose rock bottom prices.

4. Liberated Territory

A given area where revolutionary power has done away with the institutions and forces of the old regime, and where the new society is coming into being. The capitalists, landowners, and oligarchs are expropriated and held to account. The means of production are socialized, etc. From a military point of view, this assumes having both the capacity and the will to defend these zones.[24]

These categories can be all the more confusing as different authors and texts sometimes use the same terms to indicate different categories. Most of the time, Mao Zedong used the term "base of support" to mean a "stable base of support," in other words, to mean an area under total politico-military control.[25] The Vietnamese resistance referred to territory it controlled at night as "guerilla zones"—the Saigon forces remained in control during the day. In this way, many seeming paradoxes can be untangled, i.e. the recent documents by the Communist Party of Nepal which claim

24 Which does not mean that they must be defended at any cost. Liberated zones can be evacuated when faced with overwhelming military pressure. The "Long March" is an example of this.

25 The notion of "base of support" was very flexible for Mao Zedong, who spoke of "long-term bases," "temporary bases," "seasonal bases," "bases for small units," and even "mobile bases."

"not to be in a position to create stable bases of support," while at the same time stating that "a certain kind of base of support exists at Rolpa and Rukum, where we collect taxes, hold people's tribunals, control the forests, etc. [...] The police does not enter these zones." In this more than any other question, one should not fixate on the words used, but rather pay attention to the concepts being described.

Focoist analysis makes much of the fact that the Cuban guerilla did not establish a stationary base of support until more than 17 months of non-stop fighting, and blames the failure of the Peruvian guerillas in 1965 on their attempting to establish such bases prematurely. Thus focoism directly and openly calls into question the principles of Maoist Protracted People's War, according to which the creation of a base of support is the guerilla's starting point (and not some future achievement). The focoist critique not only rejects the idea (in the conditions that prevailed in Latin America in the 1960s) of trying to establish a stationary base (which would be one thing), but it even rejects the idea of depending on a "safe zone" of thousands of square kilometers. But this critique confuses the concepts *base of support* and *stationary base of support*. In actual fact, and long before the seventeenth month, the Castroist guerilla had bases of support in the Sierra Maestra. If we take the focoist critique of the base of support to its logical conclusion, we are left with nothing more than guerilla nomadism.

The experiences of those Latin American guerillas deprived of bases of support (notably the Colombian ELN in the 1960s) gave rise to the concept of *tacticism*. This refers to a situation in which isolated guerillas—either insufficiently, badly, or simply not at all supported by a political structure—lose their revolutionary value as they are forced to focus on tactical questions (provisioning, maneuvering, keeping track of what is happening on the ground, etc.) Guerillas which fall into tacticism become unable to properly carry out the necessary armed propaganda work or education of the masses, nor are they even able to develop themselves or to incorporate or train new recruits.

XIII. OPERATIONAL ART (OR THE ART OF OPERATIONS)

Strategy is mediated by operational art: if strategy determines which operations should be carried out, operational art determines the conditions under which they will be carried out. It concerns the basis and the preparation of military operations as a function of the strategic plans. As defined by Alexander Svechin, the leading Soviet military theorist of the 1920s, the operation is the means of strategy, operational art is the material of strategy; the battle is the means of the operation, the tactics are the material of the operational art. Svechin developed the concept of operational art by observing that wars were no longer settled in one big Napoleonic-style battle like they had been in the 19th century. Instead, they were decided by a series of connected operations. We can see that operational art is more relevant to guerilla strategies than to insurrectionary ones. The revolutionary forces engaged in the latter would only have use for operational art when dealing with the civil war (and/or foreign intervention) that would follow the successful insurrection.

It is obvious that what Mao referred to as the *science of campaigns*, the intermediate category between strategy and tactics, can be classified within this category of operational art.

In Maoist Protracted People's War, operational art addresses cooperation and interaction between the three levels of the armed forces: the local militias (self-defense militias), the regional forces, and the regular forces (battle corps devoted to offense, which answer directly to the general command). The guerilla's spontaneous form is that of the small fighting unit, emerging from and supported by the local population, active in the immediate vicinity from which it comes. To maintain and, even more importantly, to develop its forces, the guerilla must break with this spontaneous practice and adopt the principle of the *guerilla of movement*,[26] which falls within the category of operational art. This is a matter of bringing together fighters from different local guerilla units in order to create mobile forces which are able to spread out and move effectively over a large area (by working with local guerilla units). Such mobility

26 The term was coined by General Giap.

protects the unit (as the enemy does not know where it is), allows it to maintain the initiative (both when attacking and falling back)[27], and by being present throughout the area it reinforces the authority of the revolutionary forces. In this way the *guerilla of movement* develops into the *large guerilla*, and then reaches the stage of traditional warfare.

The principles of operational art are:

1. Mobility and the importance of accelerated rhythms in combat operations;
2. Concentrating activity at the decisive time(s) and place(s);
3. Surprise;
4. Initiative and activity in battle;
5. Preserving the capacity and efficiency of one's own forces;
6. Conformity of the operation's goals to the conditions of the actual situation;
7. Coordinating forces and methods/resources.

To present these categories more simply (and schematically), we can say that waging war is a matter of strategy, conducting campaigns is a matter of strategy and operational art, conducting battles is a matter of operational art and tactics, and that a simple armed encounter is a matter of tactics.

XIV. TACTICS

So if *strategy* determines what operations should be carried out, and *operational art* determines the conditions in which these operations are carried out, it is *tactics* that determine how these operations are carried out. Tactics is the domain of preparing and using arms, people, and methods/resources to successfully engage in an armed encounter.

Tactics possess both general and specific principles relating to different types of military operation.

---

27 To have the initiative is not the same as being on the offensive. There are hopeless offensives which reveal a lack of initiative (which are a kind of fleeing forward) as well as daring retreats through which one maintains the initiative (such as the Long March).

As we have seen, no revolutionary strategy consists of just one method, of just one tactic: for instance, the *insurrectionary strategy* not only applies *insurrectionary tactics*, but also (to a lesser degree) all of the other tactics and specific forms of the art of revolutionary warfare. To give an example, in revolutionary warfare sabotage takes on dimensions it never enjoyed in traditional warfare. It is no longer a matter of a few strategic sabotage operations decided upon by on high, but an infinite number of acts of sabotage carried out by the masses. These include actions big (putting an electrical substation out of business) and small (tearing down a government poster), and by their very number they bog down the enemy.

XV. INSURRECTIONARY TACTICS: PRINCIPLES

1. Abandon barricades in favor of small mobile groups (some of which should be specialized in anti-tank fighting) which have a good grasp of the terrain. Prepare the terrain to facilitate the action of mobile groups (make holes in the walls between houses to create passageways, etc.)
2. Use all weapons possible. In 1956, the Hungarian counter-revolutionaries electrocuted Soviet mechanized infantry by dropping tramway cables on their tanks, while the oil-soaked sheets the tanks were sliding around on made them easier to attack. In the 1946 Hanoi insurrection, the Viet Minh militias dug anti-vehicle ditches and covered them with obstacles so that the tank driver would accelerate as they approached. Use lures (decoy booby traps, decoy dugouts, etc.), obstacles (metal points dug into the ground, etc.), and traps (lay traps in areas likely to be abandoned, or even pretend to retreat in order to lure the enemy into a booby trapped area). Pay attention to the creativity of the masses and encourage the spread of useful ideas.
3. Right from the start, make the most out of the third dimension: roofs, balconies, basements, sewers.

4. Block off lines of sight (with screens hung across streets, for instance).
5. Make extensive use of snipers and ambushes and the timely setting off of booby-traps. Use methods (caches, secret passageways) that allow fighters to act in areas that the enemy believes it has secured.
6. Eventually tie up the enemy by occupying several defendable buildings (reinforced concrete, with many storeys and basements) and an open range of fire (parking lots, esplanade, boardwalk, etc.) by groups of fighters prepared to defend them to the end.

Points 5 and 6 are only justified as complementary to the mobile groups which remain the heart of insurrectionary tactics.

Initiative is the key for insurrectionary tactics. No defensive bulwark can hold out if all it does is wait for the enemy. New techniques (like systems that use microphones to capture the shockwaves from a bullet to instantaneously calculate the sniper's location) make this principle even more important.

XVI. GUERILLA TACTICS: PRINCIPLES

The struggle of the weak against the strong make guerilla tactics necessary; the general principles (valid for urban and rural guerillas alike) being:

1. Go from the simple to the complex in the organization of operations.
2. Carry out careful intelligence and reconnaissance work (time how long it will take to fall back, etc.). This can go so far as rehearsing aspects of the operation on the ground.
3. Select combatants with care and assign them their roles on the basis of their aptitudes.
4. Keep your forces hidden prior to, and in some cases during, the operation.
5. Make sure the combatants are not carrying any objects or papers that could be of use to the enemy intelligence services.
6. Make sure each combatant is completely familiar with the terrain, the objective, the unit they are in, and the action plan.
7. Know to concentrate your forces, to maneuver rapidly in the time desired.
8. Exploit the errors and oversights of the enemy.
9. Abandon (or postpone) an operation if it looks like it has been compromised (even partially) by the enemy.
10. Favor deception and mobility over firepower, while not neglecting the latter.
11. Favor ambush and surprise attacks, and ideally combine the two (ambushing units coming to reinforce the target of a surprise attack).
12. Acquire the means necessary for surprise (through the choice of objective and/or the choice of means: a target that the enemy expects to be attacked by a commando can instead be surprise attacked by a mortar).
13. Double up in order to allow new fighters to experience guerilla action without allowing for their possible shortcomings to put the operation or other fighters at risk.

14. Ensure superiority in numbers and/or resources at the time and place of the operation by employing the principle of concentrating one's forces.
15. Fall back immediately, quickly, without leaving a trace.
16. Deploy forces in order to facilitate the fall back; for example, have forces in buildings nearby prepared to treat the wounded.
17. Cover your trail.
18. Scatter your forces.
19. After each operation, have participants practice criticism and self-criticism. Communicate useful observations (mistakes to avoid, etc.) to all combatants.

XVII. TACTICS AND TECHNIQUES

Experience shows that revolutionary forces have often neglected learning certain tactics, as opposed to certain techniques. In terms of street-fighting, for instance, fighters are often taught how to handle weapons (classes about gun care, target practice, etc.) but there is a tendency to neglect teaching firearms tactics (for instance, how it is better to advance on the right side of the street, because this will mean that in order to defend themselves the enemy will have to place their weapons on their left side; in order to not expose themselves, a right-handed sniper should stick to the left side of a doorway or window). It is impossible in a presentation like this to go over all of the specific tactical principles of use in revolutionary war. These techniques are listed and described in military manuals that should be easy to obtain.

XVIII. TERRORISM

The necessity to oppose the counter-revolutionary "anti-terrorist" rhetoric is such that revolutionary forces anxious to avoid any "terrorist profile" sometimes forget that terrorism is a key element of revolutionary military policy.

It is an illusion to think that everyone will support the revolutionary project. For this reason, the revolutionary project needs to take on a didactic character: it should not only champion the historical interests of the masses, but should also be clearly seen to do so. At the same time, given the damage that can be done by traitors, infiltrators, agent provocateurs, turncoats, etc. the revolutionary forces need to benefit from their own equivalent of the "fear of the policeman" that strengthens the regime. Towards this end, deliberate counter-revolutionary activities should be punished.

Necessary though it may be, those who use terrorism should be aware of its limits. When Jerome Bonaparte, threatened by insurrection in the kingdom of Westphalia, called upon his brother Napoleon for help, he received the answer: *"For the love of God, my brother, use your bayonets!"* Jerome replied, famously, that *"You can do everything with a bayonet except sit on it."* The point being that terrorism is never sufficient, not for the counter-revolution and not for the revolution.

Nevertheless, for the revolutionary forces it does play an essential role in equalizing things. It is one of the least heroic aspects of guerilla warfare (it often amounts to executing unarmed people) and for that reason is often omitted from texts that serve (even partially) a propaganda function. Yet the numbers speak volumes. In South Vietnam, village chiefs were appointed by the Saigon authorities, and played the role of police (they were supposed to report if there were strangers passing through the village, etc.) Village chiefs who were not sympathetic to the NLF had to either be killed, or paralyzed by the fear that they might be killed. To accomplish this, a large-scale terrorist campaign was waged: between April 1960 and April 1961, 4,000 village chiefs were killed.

To the degree that they embody the interests of the people and of the proletariat, the revolutionary forces have far less need to rely on terror than do the reactionary forces. And as there is always a political price to pay for terror (it provides the enemy with a propaganda weapon), it should be measured, proportionate, and kept to a strict minimum—the example of the NLF in 1960-61 is an extreme case, as it was up against the white terror of the Diem regime.

Although the question has not been studied much, it is clear that there are consequences to not meeting the strict minimum. An American counter-insurgency expert has suggested that one of the major reasons the Red Brigades were defeated was that they did not use terrorism and had failed to intimidate the little agents of counter-revolution.

XIX. THE ART OF TRADITIONAL WARFARE (OR "BIG WAR")

As well as all this, there are also all of the specific principles of the art of traditional warfare (the necessary war of movement, and eventually the war of position) that apply to the degree that the revolutionary war develops into and takes on the methods of traditional warfare—but that is beyond the scope of this presentation.

Thank you for your attention.

Kersplebedeb Publishing and Distribution

All Power to the People
Albert "Nuh" Washington
1894820215
111 pages * $10.00

A collection of writings by the late Albert Nuh Washington, a former member of the Black Panther Party and Black Liberation Army. Washington was imprisoned in 1971 as a result of the U.S. government's war against the Black Liberation Movement. He died in prison on April 28, 2000, from cancer.

Defying the Tomb Selected Prison Writings and Art of Kevin "Rashid" Johnson featuring exchanges with an Outlaw

kevin "rashid" johnson
9781894946391 * 386 pages * $20.00
Follow the author's odyssey from lumpen drug dealer to prisoner, to revolutionary New Afrikan, a teacher and mentor, one of a new generation rising of prison intellectuals.

Divided World Divided Class: Global Political Economy and the Stratification of Labour Under Capitalism

zak cope * 9781894946414
387 pages * $20.00
Charting the history of the "labour aristocracy" in the capitalist world system, from its roots in colonialism to its birth and eventual maturation into a full-fledged middle class in the age of imperialism.

Exodus And Reconstruction: Working-Class Women at the Heart Of Globalization

bromma
9781894946421
37 pages * $3.00
An overview of the decline of traditional rural patriarchy and the position of women at the heart of a transformed global proletariat.

Jailbreak Out of History: the re-biography of Harriet Tubman

butch lee * 0973143207
87 pages * $8.00
This is a major biographical study, which refutes the standard "American" version of Harriet Tubman's life, while uncovering the significance of New Afrikan women's resistance to the developing u.s. empire.

Kuwasi Balagoon, A Soldier's Story: Writings by a New Afrikan Anarchist

kuwasi balagoon et al.
0973143282
125 pages * $10.00
The first ever collection of writings by Kuwasi Balagoon, an anarchist member of the Black Liberation Army who died of AIDS-related pneumonia while in prison in 1986.

Meditations on Frantz Fanon's Wretched of the Earth: New Afrikan Revolutionary Writings

james yaki sayles
9781894946322
399 pages * $20.00
One of those who eagerly picked up Fanon in the 60s, who carried out armed expropriations and violence against white settlers, Sayles reveals how behind the image of Fanon as race thinker there is an underlying reality of antiracist communist thought.

KERSPLEBEDEB PUBLISHING
CP 63560, CCCP VAN HORNE
MONTREAL, QC, CANADA H3W 3H8
EMAIL: INFO@KERSPLEBEDEB.COM
WEB: WWW.KERSPLEBEDEB.COM

The Military Strategy of Women and Children
butch lee * 0973143231
116 pages * $12.00

Lays out the need for an autonomous and independent women's revolutionary movement, a revolutionary women's culture that involves not only separating oneself from patriarchal imperialism, but also confronting, opposing, and waging war against it by all means necessary.

Night-Vision: Illuminating War and Class on the Neo-Colonial Terrain
butch lee and red rover
1883780004
187 pages * $14.95

The definitive analysis of postmodern capitalism, the decline of u.s. hegemony, and the need and possibilities for a revolutionary movement of the oppressed to overthrow it all.

Prison Round Trip
klaus viehmann * preface by bill dunne
9781604860825 * 25 pages * $3.00

Klaus Viehmann spent 15 years in prison for his involvement in urban guerilla activities in Germany in the 1970s. The essay is a reflection on prison life and on how to keep one's sanity and political integrity within the hostile and oppressive prison environment; "survival strategies" are its central theme.

The Red Army Faction, A Documentary History Volume 1: Projectiles For the People
9781604860290
andre moncourt & j. smith eds.
736 pages * $34.95

The first in a three-volume series, this is by far the most in-depth political history of the Red Army Faction up until 1977 ever made available in English.

The Red Army Faction, A Documentary History Volume 2: Dancing with Imperialism
9781604860306
andre moncourt & j. smith eds.
480 pages * $26.95

Covering the period immediately following the RAF's near-total defeat in 1977. This work includes the details of the RAF's activities and political evolution, how it was situated in relation to the 2nd of June Movement and Revolutionary Cells guerilla organizations, as well as all the RAF's communiqués and texts from 1978 up until the start of the 1984 offensive.

The Road Ahead and the Dialectics of Change
c. landrum * 189494626X
24 pages * $2.00

Applying the science of dialectical and historical materialism to the prison construct as it exists within the California prison system today.

"Activity in War is movement in a resistant medium. Just as a man immersed in water is unable to perform with ease and regularity the most natural and simplest movement, that of walking, so in War, with ordinary powers, one cannot keep even the line of mediocrity. This is the reason that the correct theorist is like a swimming master, who teaches on dry land movements which are required in the water, which must appear grotesque and ludicrous to those who forget about the water. This is also why theorists, who have never plunged in themselves, or who cannot deduce any generalities from their experience, are unpractical and even absurd, because they only teach what everyone knows—how to walk."
—Clausewitz, *On War*